The Cutting Edge

Poems by
Julia Vinograd

Art by Deborah Vinograd

Zeitgeist Press

cover photo: Holman Manell
art: Deborah Vinograd

ISBN: 0-929730-65-8

Zeitgeist Press
1630 University Avenue #34
Berkeley, CA 94703 U.S.A.

CONTENTS

FULL PAGE DRAWINGS

CRACKDOWN ON STREET TEENAGERS

The young street kids aren't violent
or crazy or screaming.
They just sit around cuddling puppies and each other;
they'd have to stand up to bother anyone
and it's too much trouble.
They share crumbling day-old donuts and black nail polish
and I write about them.
The city just sent a big police presence
to arrest my poems.
There's 2 cop cars on the avenue,
3 if you count the one
that went up the next block,
a pair patrolling the sidewalk
and a huge black paddywagon
that I think I saw in an Al Capone movie.
All this to arrest my poems
and I can't go downtown and get them back, eventually,
the way people do with a towed-away car.
The sidewalk is unconvincingly clear.
There should be kids in black t-shirts
and spiked leather bracelets
occasionally slapping a broken-stringed guitar.
There should be a girl with orange dreadlocks and beads
beating her small drum with her bellybutton.
There should be a boy drawing happy monsters
on the pavement with colored chalk.
The city says teenagers block doorways
and are bad for business.
But poetry is my business
and this crackdown is bad for my business.

THE JUGGLER

"I was living on Venice beach and juggling,"
he told me, "and this movie company came by
wanting to shoot homeless locals.
They were paying people so I asked the girl
how 'bout me?
She said sure but the director said
I didn't look homeless enough, no way."
I looked at him. A young guy, goodlooking,
clean ponytail, relaxed in jeans and a peasant shirt.
"They got some half-crazy guy for their movie,"
he went on, "he was coming off something
and having the shakes all over his accordion,
drooling too.
He couldn't play and I'm a *good* juggler
but he was what they wanted.
They thought he looked homeless."
The juggler shrugged, half-laughing
and tossed his sticks in the air.
They were made of recycled rubber
and his instruction booklet
claimed dropping a stick could be as enlightening
as being hit by a zen master's stick.
He wanted to sell his sticks to a new age shop;
he was free and full of future.
I wondered: for how many years
has every image of the homeless been mad, muttering,
screaming, drugged, drunk, unwashed
or at the very least terminally ugly?
With no future and a past broken into splinters
like a smashed window.
Every image, for years.
I felt I was being juggled and had just been dropped.
And the young guy's instruction booklet had it right,
it was enlightening.

3

AN EXTRA THANKSGIVING WITH A FRIEND

His old friend back east finally died
thanksgiving morning.
Four of my friends died that year.
Neither of us felt particularly thankful.
He bought an 18 pound Safeway turkey before his friend died
but his oven died
so he asked if he could roast it at my place
the day after thanksgiving.
When his friend died he phoned me, gulping sobs,
and I asked if we should cancel or freeze the turkey
and do it later.
He said "hell, no."
This was war.
He made a complete gourmet thanksgiving dinner at his place
while the turkey roasted in my oven
and brought it over as a sort of a laughing revenge.
Cranberry sauce made with sourcream
and a piece of horseradish is a weapon against god.
God can't have any candied yams,
they're for me and him and our dead friends.
2 kinds of stuffing, one with cornbread and chestnuts;
god can go eat graves.
Homemade gravy is thicker than blood.
He was practically dancing in the kitchen.
He'd brought over his grandmother's silver,
she was a great lady also dead and dining with us.
And then the turkey was glisteningly ready
and my friend had forgotten the big carving knife.
It was cold, dark and somehow not safe to leave,
he might start crying again.
All he had was a boyscout knife smaller than his thumb.
I watched his face rumpling and remembered
I'd got a black double-edged SS dagger years ago
at the flea market and had it leaning against my window

4

next to stained glass and deer horns ever since.
So we carved a thanksgiving turkey with an SS dagger,
had 2 helpings of everything and watched dumb tv
till I went into the kitchen for some reason
and started yelling. The gas was still on,
my friend has no sense of smell,
we could've joined our dead right then.
We opened windows. My friend explained about old stoves.
I wasn't listening.
God had come to our thanksgiving,
the only thanksgiving in the entire country
where he wasn't invited.
Where he wasn't welcome.
I took another spoonful of mango sherbet
biting it with all my teeth.
"I can still taste it," I whispered under my breath,
"it tastes so good."

A FAIRGROUND SHOOTING

I wasn't really listening to the news,
reassuring catastrophes, a fairground shooting,
8 people in the hospital.
The police speculated drugs or gangs or a girl
(the usual things everyone should avoid).
But then there was an official update:
an argument over a stuffed animal fairground prize
started the shooting.
I don't know what it was a prize for
or even what kind of stuffed animal.
8 people shot over Barney?
Or Garfield or Winnie-the-Pooh with a cute pot of honey
embroidered on his bib.
Which of them incited a riot?
Some shot, others trampled, all screaming.
Or a non-denominational teddybear
to keep off the monsters in bed,
has it learned the monsters so well
it can call them up?
Do we ask teddybear for monsters
when we hold his fur against our lips and whisper?
And is that whisper so loud
only guns will drown it out?
Spilled cotton-candy clotted with blood.
Drugs or gangs or a girl aren't as dangerous
(well, maybe the girl)
as those round button eyes
that stare unblinking into our own.
Lost, all lost.

SELLING POETRY

He bought my poetry book
and told me I ought to charge more than 5 dollars
and I thought that meant he liked it
and started to glow.
But no.
He had his pocket calculator out
and told me that 50 poems for 5 dollars
was 10¢ a poem and that was too cheap,
it didn't matter if the poems were any good or not.
"It does so," I sputtered, but he wasn't talking to me.
He was talking to his calculator
the two of them were making beautiful arithmetic together.
I knew he'd never read my book,
why should he?
he'd already balanced it.
I almost gave him his money back
and took the book for one of the people
who spend 20 minutes reading and then apologize
they owe their landlord 2 months back poetry,
they promised poems to a lover,
or worse, an ex-lover
and if they don't settle their poetry tab at the diner
they won't get credit at the end of the month.
They didn't need a calculator for their arithmetic,
they knew it all too well and didn't like it.
I took his 5 dollars and spent it as fast as I could
on something I didn't need,
I don't remember what.
I just wanted to get rid of it.
It felt dirty.

OLD WOMEN SELLING ROSES

Terrible old women sell funeral roses in plastic buckets
to young lovers in midnight BART stations.
Arthritic joints crackle into the soft curve of a petal.
Complaints squirm like fleas under their tongues
between "roses for the pretty lady? roses?"
as commuters wearily crowd the last train.
A raincoated crazy yells to an audience of pillars.
Underground fluorescent lights neither rise nor set.
Orange vinyl suited janitors talking baseball
mop around the lovers
till the cops close it down for the night.
But the terrible old women turn into train maps
when the cops come, except if you look close
it's maps of a junky's collapsing veins.
When the cops are gone,
old women with bulged penguin ankles
and black shawls go down another stairway
that wasn't there before.
There's a cemetery below
for all the bodies nobody found,
whose weathered stone angels have fierce bulldog faces
and the crumbling graves
are covered with chlorine-scented embalming roses
red, long-stemmed and still.

BAD TIMES

A 17 year old boy in the vacant lot
stabs a pile of dead tires
over and over, white fisted and sobbing.
Torn squelching sounds.
The tires are already too collapsed to pop.
The boy throws himself down
and a trail of ants from a nearby sunflower stalk
climb his arm. The boy doesn't notice.
A dank wind licks its lips with deadmen's shoelaces.
Cold rain has a pet name for each blind nudging earthworm
but can't tell people from stones.
The future's read in the entrails
of rusted disemboweled bicycles,
still chained to parking meters.
Stains crawl from warehouse walls,
whispering to be fed.
Mirrors snicker in doorways,
ready to leap out and mug faces.
But who has a face?
Blanks pass by.
Nobody's real but the boy,
his young mouth twisted against dirt
while the trail of ants decides a half-squashed snail
is more interesting and goes to investigate.
The boy is real.
And the blood is real.
the blood that isn't on the knife.
Yet.

CRONE

When I was about 9 I saw a silver ring
in a jeweler's window.
And I wanted it, but not to wear.
It had a small turreted silver castle on the band
and the top of the highest tower
was a dark red garnet.
I knew that garnet was the curved roof of a room
where I'd live when I was old, very old,
as old as I am now.

Everyone in the castle would be a little afraid of me
and leave my meals in front of my door
on tiptoe
and tell strangers I'd died long ago.
They'd know I watched them
when I remembered about people
which I didn't always.
What would people matter to an old woman, very old,
as old as I am now?

I'd stand at my window and raise storms,
I loved to hear the lightning laugh.
OR I'd snake my tongue out for a drop of rain
that never reached the earth
and let the fine wines sour outside my door.
I'd do magic like knitting or a jigsaw puzzle
just to keep my hand in
and the edge behind my eyes.
I'd turn the cheese in rattraps to crown jewels
just to learn new swear words from the rats.
When I was about 9 I stared at that silver ring
and saw myself an old woman, very old,
as old as I am now.

At one time I bought an identical ring,
never wore it
and watched the garnet get dusty.
It got lost when I moved.
I did learn new swear words from rats
but people still matter.
I'd like to tell that 9 year old
she's the only one
who's ever lived in that tower room.
All those cobwebbed years in the 2 minutes
she smudged her nose against the jeweler's window.

RUMORS OF WAR

Out of the rain come 2 laughing girls in leather jackets.
One has short purple hair
and a big burping rhinestone ring on every finger.
The other's black, slender, with crimson braids
wrapped in red silk and small bronze bells.
Because they have jiggling plastic earrings
and fake fur collars
we aren't going to war.
It doesn't fit in the same world.
They take their coffee outside
to smoke in the rain with a young guy
bouncing his skateboard on his knee.
And because his wrists are bright as sleepy birds
and I want to bite his adam's apple
all the children in the world have enough to eat.
2 big dogs sniff each other, barking.
Labradors, wolf-high, leaping and pawing.
They might fight like countries
but they're also wagging their tails.
I wish countries had tails.
The girl with the rhinestone rings
tears a packet of sweet-and-low in her coffee
with a purple fingernail.
Sugar is dangerous. Anthrax is dangerous.
Smoking is dangerous as they get lipstick
on their cigarettes. Time is dangerous.
And of course, it's still raining.
On sugar they agree.
Also hate.
But *they* only hate people they once loved.
Nobody else is worth the trouble.

THE LIVING ROOM COUCH

When I was growing up
there was a wine-dark velvet living room couch.
My younger sister and I used it to travel.
We'd put our hands over our eyes,
fling ourselves face down into the corners
and chant "we're go-ooooing."
Then blind and half smothered
we'd describe to each other
imaginary places, or places we'd heard about
but didn't quite believe in.
Wasn't the whole world a giant suburb
with dishwashers, guilty silences,
african violets that never quite grew,
vacuum cleaners, front lawns mowed flat
and a few flies
getting thru the porch screen door
to bang against the window till they died?
Like us?
My sister still has that couch at her studio,
worn down, sway-backed, collapsed,
at a party last year
a guest complained the sharp broken springs
almost castrated him.
We've put a blanket over the springs
but we're keeping that couch.
India is behind its cushions:
the smell of dust, spices and old copper temple roofs
turned green with time.

ON THE OTHER HAND –

Think of all the pizza places
that could live happily ever after
where you're considering
building a homeless shelter.
How can you sleep at night
imagining all those innocent little pizzas
with their round trusting faces
that need a place to stay?
Or the yogurt palaces, so sweet, so clean;
do you want their chocolate and strawberry
and natural tears to drip over everything?
How can you face yourself
if you make yogurt cry?
Doesn't the sound of their sobs break your heart?
Or the great chain of chocolate chip cookies,
so American
that if your mother didn't make them
you should send away for another mother
right now.
Aren't cookies and milk
the very emblem of a good home?
so don't they deserve a good home?
And don't you feel morally committed
to the high-rise American cookie?
                              while the homeless crumble.

BAR

The sort of dive where cigarette smoke is 3 nights old
even if he just lit his cigarette.
There are no days and everyone stays too long
on their way out.
Everyone's on their way out.
All the songs on the jukebox are slow and sad,
not that the customers loved and lost
but a broken heart is a good alibi
and the management is glad to oblige.
The waitress calls them all "dearie"
and says she has a beautiful daughter,
"she better not catch any of them
sniffing around her daughter"
and they smile
flattered to be considered dangerous
and pat her pudgy hand.
The cross-eyed motheaten moosehead is there
to look worse than the hangovers
no matter how hard the beer blows.
When the regulars talk about their lives
they're like circus barkers,
excitedly pointing inside a tent
at someone else.
A breathtaking cast of thousands
unavoidably detained
but they don't mind waiting.
They've got nothing else to do
and they'll have another drink
while they wait.

I KNOW A MAN

I know a man with highways for shoelaces,
they keep coming undone.
When he put the ocean in his pocket
an octopus ate his car keys,
he tried to explain to the policeman
pulling out various expired IDs;
it was only a small octopus,
it didn't know any better.

I know a man who sagged over cliffs,
who used his belly button for a searchlight,
who coughed up badly digested bits of clocks,
he never could keep time
down.
I know a man who laughs roller-coasters
and then falls out of them.
I know a man so sad
beetles scuttling from under garden stones
hide their armored faces from his tears.

I know a man attacked by staircases, chairs,
people on the street who look at him funny,
bureaucrats,
a striped hornet dive-bombing his room
cause he left the window open,
and beauty.
I know a man with both hands full of his heart,
it barks and beats and bites
and drips all over the furniture.

I know a man with roses in his closet,
their suffocating soft scent is plotting
to take over the world.
When he went to the circus he started on cotton candy
and ate a week's worth of fog.
He said it wasn't bad,
but he still wanted a hamburger.

I know a man who knows everything
because he sat down on it
but he won't know if it's broken till he gets up.
He's going to sit here for a while
and think about love.

FURNISHED ROOM

The walls of a furnished room aren't just walls.
They're the backs of everyone you ever wanted
turned away,
they won't look at you again.
They came all this way to lock you in
and never look at you.
The dripping faucet in a furnished room
is warm with the touch of hands
that won't touch your hands again.
There's not enough soap in the soap dish
to wash out the lies, but the truth is worse.
It usually is.
The radiator clanks unexpectedly
like someone else's ghost rattling weary chains.
You feel like telling it this room is reserved
for your ghosts but you don't speak radiator
and it probably wouldn't believe you.
There are so many beautiful people on the tv
in a furnished room, their warm caressing voices
begging you to understand
but they're the wrong beautiful people.
The tv's running on empty, the room's running on empty
and you can't run anymore.
No, you can't run anymore.

METAL PLAY

4 teenagers at outside coffee tables
playing with tin whistles:
high notes, hoots, giggles.
Straddling a chair to knock a cap off with a whistle
and claim it's an accident.
The sun's out and they're studded all over
with metal bits bright as the tin whistles.
Steel nose studs, silver hoops by lip and eyebrow;
chrome locks and chains around a throat
make flesh more fragile,
blossoming beneath the machine.
And it all shines.
Music of the immaculate misconception.
No tune and they're not looking for one.
The notes are enough. The brightness.
Needles dancing in a haystack of flesh.

JERUSALEM'S DRESS

I saw Jerusalem wearing a sequined dress.
At first I thought the sequins were stars
but they were bullets she'd polished
and set next to her skin,
bullets from lovers who died calling her name.
Any religion. Any war.
They all blew with the sand and fell in their blood.
Jerusalem kept bullets from her favorites
warm against her breasts
the way a young girl would keep a dried rose
pressed in a book of love poems.
"I can't remember them all," Jerusalem shrugged
"and I never knew their names,
they knew my name and died.
It's not my best dress," she added,
"sequins are cheap, bullets are cheaper
and it doesn't match my eyes.
But I wear it when people come to visit,
they've already got me mixed up with their dead.
Did they love each other when they were alive?"
Jerusalem asked suddenly,
pacing so the low-cut shiny bullets clicked together.
"Can they love?"
"Can you?" the Lord responded gently
and Jerusalem tossed back her smoky prayers.
"Do you like my dress?" she demanded.
"It's beautiful," said the Lord
"and it cost too much."

VIEW OF PEOPLE'S PARK

This is a doorway now, with daisies growing in it
but still a doorway, where one hides a free box
or one's shadow from a cop
or an unsuspecting wallet to be ravished,
a doorway to drink, sleep, fight,
fling out whistles
to the long-legged dares with dandelion hair,
huddle, hide, grin.
The hinges are broken and the sky leaks
but nothing's perfect.
On good days it unfolds like a child's toy,
with musicians, lovers and pictures in the smoke.
On bad days the rust shows thru.
This is a doorway creaking with birds,
with an institution green painted floor.
The lock doesn't work,
call it a park and sit down.

REMEMBERING

I remember being a young girl.
I went to an all girls high school
so I had crushes on men in books and movies.
I'd imagine a night with the Karamazov brothers
and wake up exhausted, mouth dry,
skin purpled with phantom bruises
where I was held too tight.
When I watched movies with swordfights
I'd set myself between
and make the duelers slice off my clothes.
No one could win till I was naked.
At the same time
I couldn't look at my own breasts without blushing.
I couldn't meet a casual glance.
I was ashamed of everything that hadn't happened yet,
hot fudge shame thick in my throat.
The wind was made of hands that never asked permission
or cared to know my name.
The remaining acne I hid with make-up
became love bites from men
who had to leave their mark on me.
Red, aching.
Bigger kids used to beat me up
but I was never bullied by my own body before.
Worst of all, I liked it.
I was so young.

THE FLU

It's raining inside me, it's raining outside.
I'm coughing up crowded doorways and store overhangs.
My bones ache hollow but not empty,
street people huddle inside me
to get out of the rain.
Wet clothes wrapped in plastic,
drenched day-old donuts
and when I try to move some of them start a fight.
A screaming girl scraped my throat with her nails
when she went for her lover,
he kicked my chest,
the rain washed their faces away.
Wet matches won't light a scrounged cigarette.
A 3 year old boy still believes
if he yells loud enough
someone will stop the sky to stop his noise.
They can't get away from the rain
and I can't get away from them.
Maybe it's fever. I'm sweating.
Shivering clammy hands warm themselves on my skin,
on the inside of my skin.
There's too many, I can't breathe, let me go.
A reproachful guitar starts in the snarl of my gut.
out of tune, rusted.
Sparechanging striped umbrellas worn over eyes.
I put my hands over my ears.
Enough, damn you, go away,
there isn't room for all of us
and I was here first.
It's raining inside me, it's raining outside.
The shelters are full, it's raining,
there's a flu going around the flu shots can't stop.
Will this happen to everyone?

THE STORY OF CHERRIES

I roll summer cherries in my palm,
ripeblack and much too rich
to grow on trees.
I close my eyes
and see a pirate ship after a raid,
the deck overflowing with spilled gold coins
and the king's favorite bellydancer
naked in the center
with only a ruby in her navel.
She has a suffocation of black hair
and a stilled, dangerous face like a dagger
waiting for the killing hand.
The pirates' eyes scuttle over her swaying breasts
like wasps.
The captain waves to a little man with bad teeth
hunched over a squeaky fiddle
and commands her to dance for them,
to dance first.

The ruby flashes, she leans backwards,
her slow hips clang together and apart
like a churchbell tolling for the dead.
Her raised leg points
at a gull hovering overhead;
this is the first time she's been outside
since the king's soldiers stole her.
As the dance ends she shakes her belly
and the ruby falls out,
becomes a cherry
followed by many cherries
rolling over the slippery deck.

The pirates grab them in rope-roughened handfuls,
scuffling with each other.
The cherries' skin is softer than the girl's.
The cherries' flesh is cool.
The dancer crouches, leaps, turns into a gull
and swoops off towards the sun.
The pirates yell after her
and their boots trample the cherries.
Red-purple stains everywhere
as from a bloody battle.
That's the story of cherries,
summer cherries in my palm,
not quite too beautiful to eat.

SUPPOSE A MONSTER

Suppose a monster instead of mind-numbing statistics.
Suppose a beast prowls under the city
poking its snout up thru manholes at night
and eating lost people.
Many hot teeth and scaled with mirrors.
No time to scream and no one else sees it.
But someone isn't in line for cold coffee
and colder comfort the next morning.
Forms are cancelled.
Statistics displaced by a digit.
Basically, who cares?
The beast isn't real, of course;
but the people it eats are even less real.
Half an hour later statistics get hungry again.
Soon the homeless won't satisfy the beast anymore
and the beast will go hunting.
It's gotten bigger.
And statistics can turn up anywhere,
the beast can disguise its tongue as a waterbed.
When you see your own face reflected in its scales
there's no time to scream.
You've become a statistic.

SMALL GIRL

A small blonde girl about 3 owns the coffeehouse
and passes out party favors of herself.
She appears at table's edge, a pudgy question mark
looking up under wavy bangs
and making glad, imperious squawks.
We obey.
She praises us for pleasing her,
that's what we're for.
She stamps each black and white square
of coffeehouse floor
with her floppy tennis shoes
like closing a letter with a royal seal.
Sometimes she gets bored and slips outside
running in circles, arms outstretched
and squealing *eeeeeeeeeeeeee*.
She owns the sidewalk.
She owns the sun.
She owns everything.
The world begins where she looks,
a birthday present just for her.
She's happy.
Nothing must ever change.
Nothing.

STUDENTS

They're only food for finals.
They used to have names, love lives,
lies about love lives, roommates
and midnight pizza-with-beer.
Now paper bites to the bone.
Their bloody guts re-arrange into graphs and outlines
while they're still breathing,
barely.
Students stay up all night
as the open mouths
of pale blue finals notebooks get closer
and closer.
Robins egg blue. Gentle blue.
No mercy.
If the finals like what they eat
there are happy parents and maybe jobs
at the other end of the digestive system.
If not,
then not. But in any case
the students will be eaten.
Only food for finals.
And all this time
they thought they were human.

FANTASY FOR A STATUE

I'd like to be a monument in a bad part of town
so I wouldn't be too well taken care of.
No one would scrub off pigeon droppings
or keep the metal from rusting
or keep off children who'd climb all over me
for king-of-the-mountain games and hide and seek.
Their warm round breaths never knew my name.
Not a famous monument, just a compromise
between 2 pork grabbers,
and whoever had to settle for me
probably wanted The Unknown Soldier
if they were stuck with a statue,
the first choice was a parking garage.

I'd like to be a monument in a bad part of town
avoided by garbagemen, cabbies, firemen and cops.
A man with a knife could stand behind me
so he wouldn't cast a shadow.
My nose and fingers will chip off
and I'll get splashed with red paint
and the city council will have outraged
save-the-statue meetings
because they don't want to talk about food or housing.
Public phones torn out by their roots
when guys don't like what they hear.
Wires left dangling like dead weeds.
My rusty eyes see everything.

My pigeon-spattered ears hear housewives
tapping a melon for juicy ripeness
with the precision of a banker on his safe.
A teenage flock of urban orchids heads for nightclubs

and tries to keep the whining street
from staining their leather shadows.
A circle of drunks with a brown paper bag
and everyone they used to be.
Social workers in little windows
with just-in-case wire
smiling "no" down endless lines
in several languages.
And a politician with a car microphone
loudly promising reforms: food, housing
and a parking garage. Like always.
No.

I just want to be a monument
to nothing in particular,
an eyesore sore from seeing,
my name only in pigeon language.
And the night crying on my shoulder
in a bad part of town.

STREET FIDDLER

A young black fiddler
naked except for a gold lamé loincloth
blowing in the wind, semi-egyptian,
and heavy anklets of morris bells
high stepped his way down the avenue,
jaunty hip by step and turn.
And I expected to see King Tut
tut-tutting after him.
But no one gave him more than a glance
and a nod for the fiddle work.
And suddenly I didn't want to know why.
I didn't want the fiddler to be a balancing act
between silly and a tarot card
like so much of the street.
I didn't want hungry meanings to curl around his smile
like mosquitoes.
I didn't want to see someone following him
in ordinary time passing out flyers
about a band or a rally or a reason.
I've had too many explanations;
it's like strangling in health food.
I didn't even want a poem,
he was complete in himself.
He came from nowhere, he was lovely and he's gone
cradling his old fiddle against his young neck.

"NO PETS OR CHILDREN"

Teenagers want a pet dark to take for walks
on a leash with a rhinestone flea collar.
To curl up in their laps and be stroked,
ignoring their lovers.
They want a pet dark to sniff
at their long black fingernails,
its tail in the air
curved as smoke.
They wouldn't believe in loyalty,
but they want to be permitted
the same rights as a sofa
in a room with a small dark,
a small pet dark
still too young to eat people.

APRIL FOOL

I

The April Fool somersaults everything
inside out,
outside in.
"You think I'm a stranger," says the stranger
"but april fool! I'm really your own true love
kidnapped by monsters and roses,
I'm your father and mother,
your long-lost twin brother, your dead child,
your spiritual master disguised as a beggar,
your secret spy despised as a friend,
your own face changing in the mirror
and april fool!
I'm really a stranger," says the stranger
   "and so are all of the above,
   and so are you."

II

"You think I'm a firehydrant,"
says the firehydrant
"but april fool!
I'm really buried treasure,
water locked up like money
and stolen every summer by children
with wrenches doing rain dances
to the pipes in the earth
where the washed-up sky gods hide.
I am water in love with fire,
waiting on the corner to meet my love
when the world burns
and april fool!" says the firehydrant
   "I'm really a firehydrant.
   What are you doing standing there

38

staring at a firehydrant
with your mouth open?
You're blocking traffic,
and besides, you look silly."

III

"You think I'm only fooling,"
says the April Fool
"but I'm really the dance
of telephone poles and trees behind your back
that freezes in place when you look around.
I'm really the fossil song caught inside onions
that your tears hear while I laugh.
I'm really the eyes you'll never catch
watching you,
winking in morse code,
masked in flashing lights,
the eyes you trip over everywhere
and cannot meet.
The sun and the moon are holes
I kicked in the sky.
I blew my bad breath into petal-scabbed spring
and rumpled poems
and then my best friends told me
and I brushed my teeth with death.
And april fool!"
says the April Fool,
        "I'm only fooling
        and to think you believed me.
        You believe everything.
        Don't you?
        Do you?
        April Fool!"

BUTTERFLY

A monarch butterfly lit on an open newspaper
at the sidewalk cafe,
preening its red and black wings
over the missing, presumed dead.
It didn't care, so gently.
People glancing at the paper were glad
the dead weren't anyone they knew
and where was the horoscope
and was that a butterfly?
If asked, they'd say crossly
of course they cared,
as if they'd been accused of bad manners.
The butterfly knew people
only as large, slow-moving obstacles,
less dangerous than their cars and less alive.
The presumed dead
no longer presumed anything.
The paper was reassuringly anxious
about the state of the world
but a corner of it drowned in a coffee spill.
A pretty girl saved her blue fringed scarf with a squeal.
The butterfly saved itself, gliding away
from all that sudden noise.
Nobody saved the world.

POWER FAILURE

When the power goes off
and the tv doesn't
and the light doesn't
I sit in the dark clutching a weak flashlight
and listening to ice cubes melting in my freezer.
Ancient forests might as well grow in my room.
And hibernating bears.
I'm careful where I step, not to wake them,
and I don't remember what's on the floor.
And if I shine the flashlight on the floor
I bump my shins on the dresser
and was the bathroom always this far away?
The tv is a solid obsidian rock
from a volcano that just erupted darkness
all over my room.
It's not a big power failure.
I look into other people's lit windows
putting cups in a dishwasher or studying.
A woman brushes her hair in a bright mirror.
I should've replaced the batteries in my flashlight,
it doesn't exactly shine,
it sortof takes the fifth.
Of course my clock stopped and time got out,
crawling over my skin like ants.
The manager called the electrician,
they'll check a box in the basement
where they keep the puppet strings of ordinary time
and they'll fix it.
But tomorrow, when the news is on,
and I watch the wounded in yet another little country,
wondering if I should have a sticky bun
with my morning coffee
I'll feel the puppet strings pull the back of my neck.
I'll remember the dark. Waiting.

SPRING

I want the dead to wake each year
like hibernating bears or dandelions
waving ragged suns in the drunk air,
thrusting past gravestones of cracked cement.
Black twigs send out buds
as if winter never happened.
No cold, no rain, and no one died.
not to stay silent when new kittens mewl
and even car alarms go courting.
I want the dead to wake each year
no more strange than ghostewhite plum blossoms
and as brief.
Gone in 2 weeks till next year,
making way for damp leaves
and the living.

THE MAGICIAN'S VACATION

At first he tried bartending,
it was the same kind of all-knowing,
not quite listening job.
But the drinks he poured turned into older drinks
with charms and stories.
The customers didn't mind, even an occasional curse
gave them an alibi. The owner minded.
How could he pay taxes on stock he couldn't pronounce
and didn't that 3 headed thing on the wall
use to be an elk?
For a while he was a cabbie,
he drove his fares where they really wanted to go,
this meant inventing new streets,
sometimes whole neighborhoods.
He liked people better than he had as a magician,
cabbies knew everyone was lost.
But the city bureaucrats didn't like
what was happening to their maps.
He did some time on the psychic hot line
and found out everyone was lonely.
But pale green luna moths flew out of his phone.
He thought how peaceful his enchanted cottage had been
where books of spells snored lightly
and the only people he met
were defined by some boring quest;
he'd always found them an interruption.
Of course he was going back. But there was no hurry.
Meanwhile he checked into a fading boardinghouse
and listened with appropriate respect
while Mrs. Wilshire of bobbing chins and reading glasses
told him stories of her baby granddaughter.

ENGINE

There's an engine revving up:
vroom, vroom, vroom
and I don't know if I'll drive it
or if it'll ride right over me
or both.
I can hear its throttle gunning the sky,
making our machineguns sound small
as tires going flat over a nail. Pop.
And drivers stranded in the middle of nowhere
swear helplessly.
There's a lot of nowhere in the sky.
I can hear the engine,
sometimes I hear nothing else
but I can't see it.
I don't know where it's going except fast.
Will it crash into a future
we've almost given up on
or will it just crash?
No guarantees.
And I don't know what to hold.
A steering wheel? Handlebars? Your hands?

SAXPLAYER OUTSIDE A NIGHTCLUB

Skinny old saxplayer twisted around his horn
like a bramble bush in a bowler hat in the rain.
Traffic lights turn his eyes red and green.
He's scared.
He changes with the music.
He clutches his horn like a big snake
striking his face. Saxplayer, his old bones flap
like a broken umbrella.

Hurt crashes out of his horn,
loud as a shiny red car in the movies
screeching thru a plate glass shop window.
But this is a blind warehouse district.
Iron bars on windows.
Iron bars on mirror shades.
Grime and time. His horn crashes hard enough
to bring Dead Ends back to life.
Nobody cares.
His big hands can't hold the wail;
he fails so sweetly.

Nightclub across the street plays industrial noise
with no industry.
Like a phantom amputated limb.
No jobs. No machines. No mercy.
The mirror-dark children dance,
their soft sweat stops the clocks.
No future.

Saxplayer, the storm rages out of his horn.
The no-more, not-now, go-away storm
as doors slam, as faces shut.
A child coughs the stars down into his horn,

such a quiet, terrible sound.
The song shakes his knees.
Saxplayer, he's old. He's drunk. It's raining.

In the nightclub mirror-dark children
dance in the eye of the storm.
Dance to the sound of their own skins.
Not the bands. Dance.
No hope. They don't miss it.
Now they are beautiful.
Outside the storm.
What else is there?
Only the saxplayer still fighting,
lost outside in the rain.

ALL THE WAY HOME

If I rub my bare toes back and forth
over the floorboards on this hot summer night
I can make the floorboards squeak either fast
like guilty gasping children running away
or slow like a shadow with a knife
sneaking up on me, accidentally heard.
I used to hear a sound like that
and be afraid to move.
And now my own toes cooling themselves on smoothness
make these sounds only as side effects.
I ought to feel safer,
making the sounds myself.
But I don't.
My own toes, my own little piggies
and Farmer John with a knife.

FOR JACK MICHELINE, WHO DIED

You're a rogue cab with your bellybutton
as your only headlight
speeding the wrong way thru the city's one way streets,
drunk and singing with your back seat crammed full.
There's a little old man in a porkpie hat in your back seat
cradling a goldfish bowl in one hand
and hot chicken soup in the other
and neither spills
even when you screech around corners.
But the girl in his lap screams,
her high-heeled long black stockings kicking out one window
and her long black hair whipping out the other.
There are bar stools in your back seat
with moss growing on them.
There are black beetles in your back seat
delicately exploring a squashed snail,
as dead as you are.
Yes, you're dead.
There are books and manuscripts in your back seat
piled so high
you couldn't've seen through your rear view window
if you'd ever looked back.
And you never look back.
And you never look forward.
You only go faster, except you're not driving.
You're a heavy, swaying hood ornament declaiming poems
as the whole thing goes out of control.
There are flowers and lovers and children
in your back seat about to crash out of your mouth.
And there are crucifixion nails tied to your tires
like tin cans to a wedding.
But the road can't keep up anymore.

CHILDREN AND THE MACHINE

To each half-asleep child
leaning a soft cheek on cold gears of the machine
we want to say:
"Hush, everything's all right,
the machine'll only make clever toys
for you to play with,
we won't let anything hurt you,
we'll put a little red wagon on the wheel
above your neck, oh hush."
But the words choke in our throats like tears.
They're what we wanted to hear as children
but they're not true.
"Hush," we say again, instead.
A word full of feathers and honey
in a world full of feathers and lead,
"Hush."

ANCIENT TREE

There is a tree in the middle of the city
wherever the middle of the city
is at the moment.
Its trunk's carved with initials, hearts,
death threats, all overgrown with rough bark
oozing sap and industrious wood beetles.
Unreadable, if anyone bothered.
But there's no time at the middle of the city.
Its leaves are tattoos,
drifting off the tree and dappling skin
loosely as leaf-shadow, at first.
Wind blows the tattoos: dragons, tigers,
roses, knives, naked girls, jailhouse tears.
Skulls, ships, roses, roses.
Skin is their only perfume.
It's enough.
There is a tree as old
as the young are young
when they are young forever.
There is a tree in the middle of the city
no matter what else is there,
or how soon it's gone.

STREET GUITAR

Flesh, fur, and music all mixed up.
Sweat rolls down brown shoulders thru black hair
curly around his navel.
Sweat sizzles on his guitar.
He tosses his head shaking off sounds
like a dog shakes off water.
Grinning. Biting.
Blue bottle flies hover thirsty.
His hair's unmade as this morning's bed.
Music is sticky on his dirty fingers
as black bursting plums. Bare feet.
Wriggle toes tickle a chair leg.
A woman beats on the walls of his song
with her fists, wailing to get out.
He grins, cradling the guitar.
He pretends not to hear.

53

AN OLD MOVIE

One of my favorite old movies
was playing on cable that morning.
I had a friend over bringing coffee,
warned other friends not to call,
even got someone off the phone
with a real emergency.
Then after an hour the screen went black,
the print torn, unnoticed, they didn't fix it,
all the other channels were fine.
But it wasn't reality I felt dropped back into
with a thud.
In the movie everything was perfectly balanced,
it all came out badly
the way it was supposed to.
But my life, all our random, muddled lives
are only restroom breaks for the gods,
time for them to get more popcorn and cigarettes
while we fall in love and worry about the rent.
And the gods chatter trivial gossip through our lives
the way no uniformed usher with a flashlight
would allow at a movie theatre.
The broken movie.
In the theatre silence is the hush before,
a vibrating live thing.
But after the broken movie a broken silence.
Any meaning I want
I have to make
from dust and colored pebbles.

WORLDS APART

I barely remember Ban the Bomb marches.
Hiroshima and the white outlines of bodies.
The red button.
World without end could end at any time.
Duck and cover drills in grade school.
Each blade of grass, each day,
stolen from us.
No more future. Nasty.
We were outraged but we didn't quite believe.
Mountains, after all.
Tracking back sand from the beach.
Now.
More countries flexing bombs.
Bare arms. Boasting.
I see wolves climbing a hill,
proven pack leaders
to throw back their throats
and howl with all their teeth
at the full moon.
Perfectly natural.
Beautiful in a way. And whatever happens
it's not our fault.
It's the fault of the full moon.

KITTEN

The kitten's about 6 weeks old,
riding a young girl's backpack
and making beepeling chimes of protest
at a large dog
who wants to climb up and investigate.
The dog gets larger everytime it wags its tail.
Famous coffins float thru the sky like clouds.
A 5 year old boy fiercely stalks his muffin
thru the tropical jungles of a coffeehouse.
The straw he clutches is a blowpipe.
The muffin won't escape.
The boy won't escape.
The girl with the kitten has blond dreadlocks,
a striped purple scarf holding transparencies
together at her hips and a fluttering mouth
ready to fly away.
But she won't escape either.
Funeral flowers thrown from the television
strew our footsteps, a path we won't escape.
Yes, we live forever
but we can count our forevers on both hands,
not including thumbs.
Can't we do something first?
Can't we look past our little boxes
at each other?
Large dogs wagging their tails.
Not going away.

POETRY

Poetry is the tv guide sit-com characters read
describing when *we're* on
and what happens in *our* next episode.
Poetry is a church that preys upon its god;
the soul has no time for table manners.
Poetry is dangerous, stupid and necessary,
Like us.
Poetry is a classical statue with a nosebleed.
Poetry is a comic book for prisoners of love.

A blank page is a gag over our mouths,
a jail to break out of, a white straitjacket
tying our arms tighter the more we fight.
A blank page is a tombstone to rise up from
and every day is the day of judgment.
There's no good time for poetry
and it's not something to get around to
when there's more time.
Forever is a door knocking on our eyes. Open.

Poetry's made of heaven's hangovers
and hell's abandoned hope
and the first thing seen after closing your eyes
and counting to a hundred.
Remember hide-and-seek?
We're all hiding now while poetry seeks,
we've forgotten it's a game.
We think we belong toad-huddled in dark corners
behind walls we call safety.
Afraid to be found.

Poetry is a trashcan where kids in baseball caps
aim paper airplanes,
laughing so much they usually miss.
The planes go on flying into the sun.
Save the world? Poetry creates the world.
If nobody dreams *no* dream comes true.
Poetry is a jigsaw puzzle of us,
how do we all fit together?
Old women in buses,
with grocery bags of river-rounded stones.
And the deep river flowing thru us
waiting for words.

AT A CHINESE RESTAURANT

I was with some friends and we'd just had dinner
at a very good Chinese restaurant
with cheerfully tasteless decor:
wall sized shiny postcards of Hongkong,
light-bulb chandeliers, fake red tassels.
We were leaving, laughing, warm and fed
and we saw one of the waiters on his break
standing by the restaurant wall.
He was skinny, sober, hobbled in kitchen whites
and singing softly to the night.
To the rain. In his own language.
The song was thin and delicate
undeniable as the rain
and the rain answered him.
Like calligraphy.
Precise brushstrokes demanding space.
The page was complete: night, rain, him.
We weren't written.
There wasn't room.

LONELY

Lonely phoned when you were out,
that's why the red light's flashing
but he didn't leave a message.
You knew it was him, didn't you?
Lonely goes to the hospital for culture
in his best gloves, the way high society
goes to the opera.
Lonely sponsors all the warm tv families
you don't have. Lonely's got milk,
what do you have?
People walk through the city, carefully
not looking at each other,
shadows slammed shut as doors,
each one breathing only his own air.
Neon signs make too much noise
and no one answers.
Lonely didn't go to the concert
but once he bought scalps from a scalper,
he was trying to broaden his interests
but it didn't work.
He turns watches into pitbulls. They bite.
He bets on them and wins
and is disappointed.

VALENTINE

I bought a rose, a red, red rose,
put it in a bottle and threw it out to sea.
Whoever finds it, there is no map,
no buried treasure, no secret decoder ring,
no invisible ink.
What's written on a rose, scented, long-stemmed
is easy to read.
If you look past the rose and see our battleships
ready to bomb the hanging gardens of Babylon
the rose is still there, cupped in your palm.
If the bottle breaks on the craggy rocks of Ireland
where the singing dead have no mercy
the rose has no mercy.
Love has no mercy.
If the rose washes up, living, in the Dead Sea
touch it with living hands.
Never take it to a grave.
Follow the curl of the partly open petals
with one finger. Gently.
The rose changes nothing.
Expect nothing.
It's for you.

PUNK GIRL

I saw a girl, about 19.
She looked held together with staples and scotch tape.
If she jumped suddenly
out of the way of a skateboard
or even laughed
without warning her mouth
her arms would float down the street one way,
her legs the other,
and her head would sail off
like a startled balloon with lavender hair.
Lines of steel nose studs,
silver eyebrow rings, even tattoos
heaver than her skin.
A tarantula used its 8 angry legs
to keep her neck from being iridescently elsewhere
like a dragonfly.
Her head was bursting with hummingbirds
and only barely anchored
by neon green skeleton rubber earrings
that glowed in the dark.
She'd had the law of gravity
as a homework assignment
but she didn't always do her homework.
Without the fisherman's wire net of studs and chains
flowing over her skin
she'd crest like a bright wave
and crash back to the sea.

THE LEOPARD

A leopard paces behind the tv screen.
His sleek body curls under a rain of fake bullets
or fake rain.
The leopard isn't hunting us
or the flickering tv people
but he is hunting.
Soundlessly leaping over a screeching car chase
or padding privately thru lovers' bedrooms.
In the middle of a bullying commercial
I hear the leopard sniff the air,
nostrils flaring.
Or a tail flicks against a newsman's microphone
for a burst of static, quickly controlled.
It's very late.
The leopard's spots swim before my eyes.
I can't meet his eyes. I need glasses.
The leopard hunts what I should be hunting
instead of watching tv.
Hungry. Hungry.

GHOSTS

The tall, heavy-set guy with too much hair
whose back I just saw from a bus
has his own story, his own problems
and his own life to muddle thru
but my breath catches in my throat anyway.
I don't care who he is, I care who he isn't
and I swallow back the dead name I was about to call
like a cold stone.
It's not his fault he isn't you.
I've reached an age where there's quite a jostling crowd
of healthy backs.
Seeing them makes me so happy
at first.
It was all a mistake,
they're not really dead. But they are.
Then I hate the strangers
who take my friends' bodies in vain,
like the Lord's name;
their backs should be washed out with soap.
It's got to be somebody's fault
because it hurts so much.
Those backs died but the dead walk in sunlight
going shopping.
So many strangers don't even know their backs are dead,
don't they feel crowded?
I feel crowded.
And when the bus passes there's no real resemblance,
there never is.
But the stone is still in my throat.
The cold stone.

THE MONSTERS

I used to have a teddybear to hold at night
and keep me safe from the monsters
and tell me everything's all right.
Now I've got a paperback horror novel
full of spurting blood
and choked off screams and monsters
to read at night with the bedside light on
and tell me everything's all right;
I can always close the book
and leave the monsters trapped
inside the cage of my attention,
helpless to get out.
It doesn't keep me safe.
Neither did teddybear.
Sometimes I feel a monster reading the paperback
over my shoulder and laughing silently.
It doesn't have claws or slime-covered tentacles
or too many teeth.
It doesn't need them.
I never glance up
but I know what it looks like,
it looks like me.

SHARING

So many things divide us:
gang wars, holy wars, generic wars like generic beer
where blood is the brand name.
We forget the one thing we share:
we all live, but not forever.
Lazarus never wrote a book
about death on 10 dollars a day.
Teenagers don't believe they can die
and dress like drunken undertakers.
And there's always revenge
where we want the villain alive again
to know we killed him.

Sleeping Beauty pricked her thumb on a needle
and slept for 100 years.
I pricked my thumb on a needle
and had to get a tetanus shot.
Hot, throbbing, they gave me purple antibiotics
and told me I could've died.
We all live, but not forever.
I've watched a forest of thorns grow between us
but it's no enchantment.
we just don't want to look.

We still pretty much assume the earth is flat,
we couldn't walk if our feet believed it was round.
And we still pretty much assume
we'll wake up in the morning
otherwise we'd never close our eyes.
I took my thumb home and scolded it.
I was ashamed, surely a person
commands the loyalty of their own thumb.
No.

No ideas.
Morning dew on a lawn before the colors come.
The shiny rubbed arms of an old plush chair.
A swinging porch screen door with a few flies.
A lullaby.
We all live but not forever.
Remember.

UNDESIRABLES

Teenagers sprout from cracks in the sidewalk
like weeds. Pliant, pushy.
Merchants want sidewalks paved over
and people without roots
pulled out by their roots.
Kittens, spikes, piercings, puppies.
Merchants worry about tattoos.
Does writing on bodies lead to writing on walls?
Is there a clear and present danger
of tattooed dragons burning their window displays?
Can tattooed pirate ships sink merchant ships
with their holds full of keychains
and souvenir ashtrays?
Teenagers wear leather jackets
over a public disturbance of soft and warm.
Teenagers wear chain necklaces bolted over smooth throats.
Chain stores. Locked out. Locked in.
They're a skinny, damp-palmed sprawl
playing peek-a-boo with death
and blocking the doorways.
A girl with purple hair lost her bellybutton ring
and wants the others to help her look.
No one pays much attention.
Night's coming and they're all out of cigarettes.
They talk about clubs and bands but it's just talk.
If there were light they might be lovely.
If there were time they might be young.

Julia Vinograd is a Berkeley street poet. She has published 44
books of poetry, and won the American Book Award of The
Before Columbus Foundation. She has a poetry tape out
called *Eye Of The Hand*. She received a B.A. from the
University of California at Berkeley and an M.F.A. from the
University of Iowa.

Selected titles available from Zeitgeist Press:

Where's My Wife by **Jennifer Blowdryer** $3.00
Wrong Wrong Wrong by **Jennifer Blowdryer** $3.00
Trek To The Top Of The World by **Andy Clausen** $3.00
Without Doubt by **Andy Clausen** $5.95
The Cities Of Madame Curie by **Laura Conway** $4.95
My Body Is A War Toy by **Joie Cook** $3.00
As Luck Would Have It by **Eli Coppola** $3.00
As For Us by **David Gollub** $5.00
Special Effects by **David Gollub** $3.00
how sweet it is by **q. r. hand, jr.** $3.00
The Satin Arcane by **Jack Hirschman** $3.00
Bad Dog Blues by **Bruce Isaacson** $4.95
love affairs with barely any people in them
by **Bruce Isaacson** $5.95
Going For The Low Blow by **Vampyre Mike Kassel** $3.00
Wild Kingdom by **Vampyre Mike Kassel** $3.00
Kept In The Pocket Of My Poems by **Paul Landry** $3.00
The Queen of Shade by **Sparrow 13 LaughingWand** $3.00
Imaginary Conversations With Jack Kerouac
by **Jack Micheline** $5.00
Outlaw Of The Lowest Planet by **Jack Micheline** $5.00
Cabaret Noir by **Delta O'Hara** $3.00
American Romance by **Eliot Schain** $3.00
Slow for a Mania, Fast for a Waltz by **Peter Tenney** $3.00
The Blind Man's Peep Show by **Julia Vinograd** $4.95
Blood Red Blues by **Julia Vinograd** $4.95
A Door With Wings by **Julia Vinograd** $4.95
Speed Of Dark by **Julia Vinograd** $4.95
Evil Spirits and Their Secretaries by **David West** $3.00
Corpse Delectable by **Danielle Willis** $4.00
Dogs In Lingerie by **Danielle Willis** $5.95
Tenderloin Rose by **Kathleen Wood** $3.00

Zeitgeist Press
1630 University Avenue, #34
Berkeley, CA 94703 U.S.A.
please add $1 per book for handling and postage